STAR GATE
ASCENSION

greater usefulness in His Gospel work. Like a blacksmith who plunges the raw steel into the hot coals so that he might make something more beautiful and useful; so too has my Heavenly Father plunged me into life's furnace. So that He may mold me into a useful and beautiful tool in His hands.

Shannon Horst
shannon.horst@icloud.com

God and Father of our Lord Jesus Christ, the Father of Mercies and God of all comfort, who comforts us in all our afflictions, so that we may be able to comfort those who are in any affliction, with the comfort with which we ourselves are comforted by God". I was, and continue to be, comforted; so that I would comfort others.

Life has certainly exposed many of my great weaknesses, but now I join Paul in boasting in them. I am fully aware of the failures of my past, and of my weaknesses that contributed to those failures. But in my weakness, Christ's power can take my story and work mighty deeds. From time to time, I'll be asked to preach and each time I do I make it a point to be as authentic and vulnerable as I can. I want each congregation to see a broken man clinging to Jesus, because that is what I am. That is what we all should be. This standard of holiness that we are called to is impossible to meet on our own. When we see such a high standard of holiness, we have no choice but to admit our weaknesses and cling to Jesus. He is our holiness; through Him we meet the impossible standard. I also have an opportunity to be a part of a motorcycle ministry, where I have been teaching weekly Bible studies. The motorcycle culture, in many ways is a marginalized group. Men and women written off because of the way they look, or act or even prejudices others may hold. The Lord has called and qualified me to reach this sub-culture, of which I am a part. Here I can again put my weaknesses on display for the Glory of God and bring comfort to hurting people. I would have never chosen this path that I am on. My life is certainly not like anything I would have imagined when I was younger. Yet, this is the path that my Lord has me on. While it is painful and most times confusing, I trust that the Lord is doing something spectacular with my life. He is preparing me for

I was far from it. Certainly, there is a balance to this, but I have been intentional about sharing my weaknesses with others. I have a new appreciation for what Paul wrote, "But he said to me, "My grace is sufficient for you, for my power is made perfect in weakness." Therefore, I will boast more gladly of my weaknesses, so that the power of Christ may rest upon me" (2 Corinthians 12:9). I once made my life about showing people how strong and capable, I was, it's no wonder that I could not sustain the illusion. Paul was most effective when he admitted his weaknesses and leaned into the strength of the Lord. When we humble ourselves enough to admit that only the Lord can sustain us we're given great freedom and power. In our brokenness, we are most effective. I have also come to understand that I cannot do this alone. So, I have surrounded myself with trusted friends who are invested in my life and in my sobriety. This seems to be a by-product of vulnerability. When I started opening to friends and family, I found that they naturally wanted to support me. It seems that it not only "takes a village to raise a child" but it takes a village to support an addict. And I will forever be grateful for my village.

Through it all I still feel compelled to preach the Gospel of Jesus Christ. I pray that one day He would see fit to place me in vocational ministry once again. Where once I saw shame and failure, now I see preparation through pain. The experiences that I have had and the pain that I have felt has uniquely qualified me to reach others who may be feeling as hopeless as I once did. When I came to the end of myself, broken, living in a homeless shelter I was comforted by the Lord. Now I see that those experiences and the comfort I found was given to me so that I might comfort others in the same way. The Apostle Paul spoke of this very thing in 2 Corinthians 1:3-4 (ESV), "Blessed be the friendships with some of the men there, relationships that I would have never otherwise had. I remember years ago, praying that the Lord would open my eyes to the hurting. I prayed that the Lord would give me opportunities to reach the "least of these". Years later, I found myself literally among them. The catch though, was *I was one of them*. I was not a "white knight" riding in to save them, I was broken and hurting just like them. My time at Bethesda was invaluable, and I count it as one of the most valuable experiences I have ever had. I saw the Gospel not only as something to be proclaimed to others, but as a soothing balm for my own soul. My counselor once said that I was good at reading Scripture, but he followed with "you're not very good at allowing Scripture to read you". It is a subtle difference, but his words impacted me deeply. During my time in the mission, I began reading the Word differently. Reading the Word prayerfully. Pleading with the Lord to allow His Word to penetrate my own heart first, before trying to disperse it to others.

When I returned home, I found it to be a completely different place than the one I left. My behavior of the previous years had damaged my marriage and drove a wedge between me and my two oldest children. Yes, there is healing from addiction, but there will always be consequences. It was not long before I was asked to leave the house for good. So, I found myself homeless once again. I lived in my pickup for a little over two weeks, then my parents took me in for a time until I found the apartment that I live in now. I have been completely sober since September 11, 2018 and with the Lord's help I will stay that way. I have begun discovering different coping mechanisms to remain in recovery. As strange as it seems, the most effective way I've found is: vulnerability. So much of my life in ministry was spent hiding my emotions, telling people I was "fine" when

STAR GATE ASCENSION

The Cure to Boredom and World Disease

by
Kosol Ouch
and
The Traveler Team

E-BookTime LLC
Montgomery Alabama

STAR GATE ASCENSION
The Cure to Boredom and World Disease

ISBN: 1-932701-71-0

Published January 2005
E-BookTime, LLC
6598 Pumpkin Road
Montgomery, AL 36108
www.e-booktime.com

Printed in the United States of America

Contents

I. Introduction

Greetings dear souls, my name is Kosol Ouch and I am 31 years of age. For the past several years I have been researching and developing a project called the Star Gate. What is the Star Gate? It is a doorway or pathway into another world, another reality, an entirely different realm of existence beyond this third dimensional plane of existence. Star Gate travel was inspired by the movie and mini series by the same name. The basic mechanics of the techniques were given to me by my guardians and the angelic guardian force. After learning the techniques I have spent the past few years using them to facilitate Star Gate travel, and now I pass this knowledge on to you. Use these techniques to help yourself grow and learn spiritually, and to help others discover their true nature as multi-dimensional beings.

The essence of Star Gating is simply shifting your awareness to other levels and realms of existence. Star Gate traveling can be likened to induced astral travel or lucid dreaming. The idea is similar in that you are accessing another level of awareness and existence which is normally inaccessible through the typical modern lifestyle. It is different, in that it does not take months or years of study, practice, or application in order to be experienced (as might astral travel or lucid dreaming). The Star Gate facilitator is like a conductor of energy which is channeled directly to the travelers. The mechanics of facilitating are very simple and there is no prior knowledge or experience that the traveler needs. The travel happens automatically and the only requirement is that the traveler maintains direct contact with the facilitator, that's it! Other methods, techniques, and paths of spiritual development may take months, years, or a lifetime to obtain any progress or results. This is the short road to spiritual development and it is time for people to start walking it.

The purpose of this information is to help awaken individuals to their inherent nature as spiritual beings having a human experience. Multi-dimensional existence is the fabric of your being, and you are simply living and perceiving one aspect of it at this very moment. Most religions, philosophies, and now science, are tapping this same well of knowledge to some degree, they are simply expressing it in different terms, concepts, contexts, and perspectives. Exploring and developing a higher awareness of this concept will reveal to you the natural order of the universe. We are currently living in a time of great spiritual awakening on this planet, and the Star Gate method of meditation will help facilitate and speed up this awakening. We are living in a very exciting and historic time right now as planet earth herself is awakening to ascend into higher dimensions of existence.

For those who enjoy their conditioned way of living and are threatened by any new knowledge, go back to sleep. For those who reject the exploration of new ideas and experiences, then this book is probably not for you. Otherwise, you have picked up this book because you know there is something more to life than what you've been led to believe exists. Whether you are just beginning your spiritual journey or are a seasoned student of the soul, you will gain from the knowledge that these pages contain. Use the techniques and experiences shared in this book to supplement your journey, and to help others begin their own journey. This being said I invite you with an open mind and open heart to explore the beauty, mystery, and infinite nature of your multi-dimensional existence. Re-discover the majestic sovereignty of your true self and your limitless god like potential which is just waiting to be unleashed. Discover just how deep the rabbit hole really goes........

II. Key Concepts

Before getting into the mechanics and techniques, you need to be aware of some key concepts that deserve a constant awareness throughout the entire process. These will help speed up the process of not only your spiritual evolution, but the effects and benefits you will gain from Star Gate travel.

Paradigms and Belief Structures

First you must let go of any conditioned beliefs you may have about what is real vs. not real, true vs. false, and right vs. wrong. Bringing any kind of pre-established belief structure into the Star Gate method will only hinder your growth and progress. Creativity is essential in exercising the potential of your mind, so simply be open to new information and ideas. Experience is the true teacher, so take what you learn and then integrate that into your belief structure. Some of your existing beliefs may collapse, change, or expand based on what you learn from this book, but don't shut out any possibility and stubbornly hang on to just one idea or belief. What beliefs do are cause expectations. Once you have a set of expectations and they are not met, then you begin to either doubt your beliefs or rationalize them. If you doubt your beliefs, then you create inner and personal confusion and a distrust of anything new. If you rationalize your beliefs based on expectations that are not met, you are simply perpetuating a structure you need in order to validate your own beliefs and ideas. The answer to this is simply let go of any beliefs and expectations. Do not create any state of mind that will set you up for disappointment. Remember this is a learning and growing experience. This is not to say that belief is not important, this is not the case at all. Belief, like truth, is a dynamic concept, not a static one. Your beliefs and concepts of truth will grow as you learn and grow. Simply keep an open mind and be willing to observe and integrate all your experiences into a self validated foundation of knowledge that you can grow from. Never follow anyone's words with blind faith including the words in this book. Simply be receptive to all knowledge and validate for yourself what is real and true. Self validation is extremely important when walking the path of enlightenment.

Visualization

Visualization, imagination, and creativity are very important when learning anything new. You must be able to open your mind to all possibilities otherwise all you are doing is creating blocks in your thought pattern that limit your potential. When you travel through the Star Gate, visualization and imagination are very important. You must be able to open your mind to a new level of perception, one that is beyond your normal five senses. This process is nurtured by the ability to create visual images in your mind and imagine them with full and vivid substance. The key to giving your thoughts substance is through the power of emotion.

Emotions

Emotions are another important concept that need to be touched on. Your emotions are a double edged sword and can have a great impact on yourself and those around you. If you radiate love and compassion then you will notice this in your thoughts, your ideas, and your physical, mental, and spiritual well being. You will find that the actions you take are more rational toward personal growth and development and you will be healthier both mentally and spiritually. If you consistently focus upon hate and negative emotions, you will equally reflect this in your physical, mental, and spiritual well being. This can result in negative actions that harm yourself and/or others, and can result in personal depression and lack of spiritual enlightenment. Always keep an open mind and an open heart. Be willing to accept that all you will learn and experience are for the greater good of your own growth and development. As you grow, you will begin to understand that even the most heinous of crimes are necessary in order to strike a balance. Love cannot be known, unless you know what lack of love is (hate), and vice versa. Love, compassion, and trust are especially important when you facilitate and travel through the Star Gate, especially (as mentioned above) when combined with your visualization. This is what will give your experiences the reality you need for self validation.

Safety and Common Sense

Please understand that this is a serious process and should be undertaken with the utmost commitment to safety. When someone travels, they are having an out of body experience (OBE). Use common sense, and never do anything to endanger the facilitator or traveler. For example, never break contact while someone is traveling. Their soul may never find its way back to the physical body, resulting in a third dimensional death of the body. Also, shaking or yelling at a traveler while they are having an OBE may cause shell shock, or psychic shock. The effects of this could range from temporary disorientation, to actual negative physical side effects. Simply put, understand that you are dealing with people and their energies and this must be approached with complete seriousness. Just like when you are driving friends in a car, their life is in your hands and you pay careful attention to where you are taking them for a safe journey. This is no different. I will speak to some more specific issues of safety in another chapter, but keep this in mind for now.

Your Guardians

Everyone has guardians that watch over them from a higher dimension of existence. You can call them your guardians, guardian angels, spirit guides, or whatever you like. Regardless of what you call them they are there to help and protect you. They can help during the process of Star Gate meditation and I will make mention of them throughout the book.

Universal Rule

One more simply profound concept is the universal golden rule. That is, *do no harm to yourself or to others.* This is a free will universe and no one has the right to force, manipulate, or control anyone else. Each person is their own sovereign being and has the right to exist and walk their own path as long as this path does not involve harming themselves or others. Remember this, and you will be just fine.

III. Mechanics

The mechanics of the Star Gate method are extremely simple and I will now explain how it works. The meditative method is the source of the entire Star Gate method, as well as all the related methods that one can use if for. This will all be explained in more detail throughout the book, but let's start with the core mechanics.

One very important thing to keep in mind is that you must have compassion and good intent. Compassion is what gives substance to your visualizations. In other words when you visualize something, it is your love, trust, and compassion which give it substance. This brings up another important point which is visualization. You must use your powers of visualization, imagination, and creativity in order to maximize your results. Finally, keep an open heart and open mind, and proceed with the meditative method as follows:

Preparation

1. Find a comfortable position to sit in. You may sit in a chair, or on the ground kneeling, in a half lotus sitting position, or even laying down. The important thing is that you are comfortable, and try and keep your back straight.

2. Rest your hands with your palms facing up (relax your hands, don't stretch them out all the way), and touch the tips of your thumb and index together. (it doesn't matter where your hands are, just that your hands and arms are relaxed and comfortable)

3. Relax and close your eyes.

4. Touch your tongue to the roof of your mouth. This creates a circuit of energy and can help ground your energy during this exercise. It can be any part of your tongue, making contact with any part of the roof of your mouth, as long as it is comfortable and not distracting. ****Always try to keep your tongue in contact with the roof of your mouth throughout the entire process**

5. Now, visualize a sun or ball of energy about the size of a basketball. Place this sun about 4-6 feet above you. Make sure you have a good idea of where the sun is, and what it looks like. It can be any color or colors. Imagine it is radiating with light and energy.

6. Next visualize another sun, again the size of a basketball. Place this sun 4-6 feet below you. Again, just be aware of where it is, and what color(s) you choose to make it. Imagine it is radiating with light and energy.

7. Now, visualize a 3rd sun. This sun is about the size of your fist and will be located in your higher chest area between the 4th and 5th chakras. This area is often referred to as the soul seat. The color of this sun can also be any color(s).

These are the preparatory stages to the Star Gate meditation. I will now explain the actual method once you have comfortably and confidently prepared yourself with the above 7 steps. (For the sake of simplicity, I will refer to the visualized sun that is below you as the 1st sun, your higher chest/soul seat sun as the 2nd, and the visualized sun above you as the 3rd sun.) Now proceed with the following (remember, tongue always to the roof of your mouth):

Lower Sun

1. Inhale slowly and deeply through your nose, and imagine that a beam of liquid light is beaming from the 1st sun (below you), straight into the 2nd sun (soul seat). Imagine the 2nd sun collecting this energy, as it also radiates light and energy.

2. Hold your breath for 3-5 seconds and while you are holding your breath, imagine that the 2nd sun holding that energy and intensifying.

3. Exhale through your nose, and as you do focus only on the 2nd sun. Imagine that is rotating while radiating light and energy in all directions. It can rotate in whatever direction you choose.

4. Do this 20 times.

Higher Sun

5. Inhale slowly and deeply through your nose, and imagine that a beam of liquid light is beaming down from the 3rd sun (above you), straight into the 2nd sun (soul seat).

6. Hold your breath for 3-5 seconds and while you are holding your breath, imagine that the 2nd sun is holding the energy and intensifying it.

7. Exhale through your nose, and as you do focus only on the 2nd sun. Imagine that is rotating, and radiating light and energy in all directions. Remember, it can rotate in whatever direction you choose.

8. Do this 20 times.

Holding Breaths

The holding breath is a focus strictly on the 2nd sun in your soul seat, the one that you just charged up with all that energy. What you are doing is simply focusing on this energy now in order to contain and intensify it.

9. Inhale slowly and deeply through your nose while focusing on the 2nd sun.

10. Hold your breath for 3-5 seconds and imagine the sun rotating in the direction of your choice.

11. Exhale through your nose, and as you do imagine the continuing to rotate while radiating light and energy in all directions.

12. Do this 20 times.

Cooling Breaths

The cooling breath is simply a focus on the 2nd sun, after drawing in all that energy into it. During this phase you are slowly releasing all the energy you just collected.

13. Breath normally now, but have an awareness of your breathing. Make sure it is deep, relaxing, and controlled.

14. As you breath focus only on your 2nd sun. Imagine it rotating and radiating light and energy in all directions.

15. Do this 40 times.

This, dear souls, are the basic mechanics for the Star Gate meditative method. As you can see it is really quite simple. It involves creating a ball of light and energy (a sun) in your soul seat. Then, draw up energy (symbolizing the earth) into your soul seat. Next, draw down energy from the higher sun (symbolizing the heavens) into your soul seat. Finally, focus on the energy you have collected and imagine it simply rotating and radiating light and energy. And of course your tongue must always be touching the roof of your mouth. That's it! Do you see how easy the mechanics of the meditative method is? I will now expand upon this a bit and explain how to use this method to facilitate Star Gate travel.

IV. The Facilitator

The facilitator is the person who plays the key role in Star Gate travel. Without them, the entire process is not possible. The facilitator acts as a conductor of energy, where energy is collected into their body and then passed on to the travelers. They are taking this energy from the Universal Energy Field (UEF) and bringing into their bodies, which then raises the molecular vibration of the travelers so they can experience the effects of Star Gate Travel. Simply put, the facilitator is like a battery which powers the entire operation.

** Since the facilitator is similar to a battery, they can only provide a certain amount of energy. It is best practice to only have 1-2 travelers for 1 facilitator. The process can be very draining indeed for the facilitator because each traveler needs a different amount of energy to travel. Therefore 1-2 travelers for 1 facilitator is the best ratio.

Being a facilitator is very simple and involves all the mechanics described earlier. There are, however, a couple variations that are included specifically for the role of the facilitator. For the ease of your reference I will include the entire meditative method once again but include the parts specific to the facilitator.

Preparation

1. Find a quiet a comfortable place where you will not be disturbed or distracted. Make sure that all cell phones, televisions, and telephones are turned off. Minimize distraction and maximize isolation.

2. Find a comfortable position to sit in. You may sit in a chair, or on the ground kneeling, in a half lotus sitting position, or even laying down. The important thing is that you are comfortable, and try and keep your back straight.

3. Relax your hands and arms, and place your hands somewhere comfortable with the palms facing up. Touch the tips of your thumb and forefinger together.

4. Next, your traveler(s) must maintain direct contact with you. Make sure they are also comfortable and in a position to place their hand on you. Their hand should be placed on your leg, your knee, or thigh. (skin to skin contact works, or if there is clothing (pants or stockings) then that is fine as well. It makes no difference, as long as there is direct contact made.)

5. Tell your traveler(s) to just close their eyes and relax. Wait until they are comfortably positioned and ready to begin.

6. Ask your guardians for a safe and fulfilling experience, and thank them for their help.

7. Now, relax and close your eyes.

8. Touch your tongue to the roof of your mouth.

9. Visualize a gate in front of you. This gate must be big enough for someone to walk through. It can be of any shape or color you wish. It may be a circular gate made of stone, or a square doorway made of

wood. The important thing is that you create a gate of your liking, and make sure it is the proper size.

10. Now imagine the gate coming alive. You can pretend the gate filling with liquid energy, or becoming a swirling vortex. Regardless, imagine that the gates are now activated and ready to transport the traveler(s).

** Note that you may create as many gates as you like but must be able to maintain an awareness of where each one is!! It is a best practice to start with 4 gates. One in front of you, one behind you, one above you, and one below you. They can be facing in any direction but you always want to maintain an awareness of your gates. During the meditative process you may want to just pause with your eyes still closed, and just look around to make sure you still have an awareness of your gates and where they are. Then continue where you left off.

11. Now, visualize a sun about the size of a basketball. Place this sun about 4-6 feet above you. Make sure you have a good idea of where the sun is and what it looks like. It can be any color or colors. Imagine it is radiating with light and energy.

12. Next, visualize another sun again the size of a basketball. Place this sun 4-6 feet below you. Again, just be aware of where it is and what color(s) you choose to make it. Imagine it is radiating with light and energy.

13. Now visualize a 3rd sun. This sun is about the size of your fist and will be located in your higher chest area between the 4th and 5th chakras. This area is often referred to as the soul seat. The color of this sun can also be any color(s).

14. Touch your tongue to the roof of your mouth. This creates a circuit of energy and can help ground your energy during this exercise. It can be any part of your tongue making contact with any part of the roof of your mouth, as long as it is comfortable and not distracting.

Lower Sun

15. Inhale slowly and deeply through your nose, and imagine that a beam of liquid light is beaming from the 1st sun (below you), straight into the 2nd sun (soul seat).

16. Hold your breath for 3-5 seconds and while you are holding your breath, imagine that the 2nd sun is holding and intensifying the energy you just beamed into it.

17. Exhale through your nose, and as you do focus only on the 2nd sun. Imagine that is still rotating, and radiating light and energy in all directions. Remember, it can rotate in whatever direction you choose.

18. Do this 20 times.

Higher Sun

19. Inhale through your nose, and imagine that a beam of liquid light is beaming down from the 3rd sun (above you), straight into the 2nd sun (soul seat).

20. Hold your breath for 3-5 seconds and while you are holding your breath, imagine that the 2nd sun is collecting and holding the energy while intensifying it.

21. Exhale through your nose, and as you do focus only on the 2nd sun. Imagine that is rotating and radiating light and energy in all directions. Remember, it can rotate in whatever direction you choose.

22. Do this 20 times.

Holding Breaths

The holding breaths are identical to the previous methods of drawing energy from the lower sun and higher sun. The only difference is that you are no longer drawing in energy. You are simply focusing on the sun you have created in your soul seat area, to contain and intensify all the energy you just collected. The process is as follows:

23. Inhale slowly and deeply through your nose, and as you do focus on the 2nd sun (soul seat).

24. Hold your breath for 3-5 seconds, and as you do imagine the 2nd sun rotating, and radiating with light and energy.

25. Exhale through your nose, and as you do continue to focus on the 2nd sun which is rotating and radiating with light and energy in all directions.

26. Do this 20 times.

Cooling Breaths

The cooling breath is simply another focus on the 2nd sun after containing all that energy during the holding breaths. You are still only maintaining your focus on the 2nd sun, but now you are breathing normally. No more slow inhalations, breath retentions, or slow exhalations. Breathe as you normally do, just make sure it is deep and relaxing.

27. Breath normally now, but have an awareness of your breathing. Make sure it is deep, relaxing, and controlled.

28. As you breathe focus only on your 2nd sun. Imagine it rotating, and radiating light and energy in all directions.

29. Do this 40 times.

Awakening the Traveler

When you are done, you may continue again from the beginning if you wish. (lower sun, higher sun, holding breaths, cooling breaths). This simply allows for the traveler to have more time. If, however, you are feeling drained or exhausted, or simply wish to end, then it is time to awaken the traveler.

To awaken the traveler you must do so in a calm and gentle fashion. Do so by tapping them on the hands, on the knees, and on the legs. Tapping and rubbing the bottom of the feet also have a ground effect, and help to awaken the traveler. The purpose is so ground the traveler back into this reality so they can regain their bearings, re-collect their thoughts, and then share their experiences.

** *NEVER* tap the head, this is dangerous for the traveler may result in injury. This is a very sensitive area.

Step 1

The Facilitator

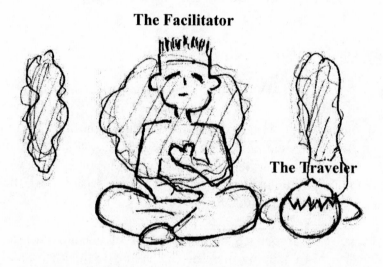

The Traveler

Visualize/open three or more gates (on the sides/front). The traveler lies next to the facilitator with one hand on the facilitator's knee.

Step 2

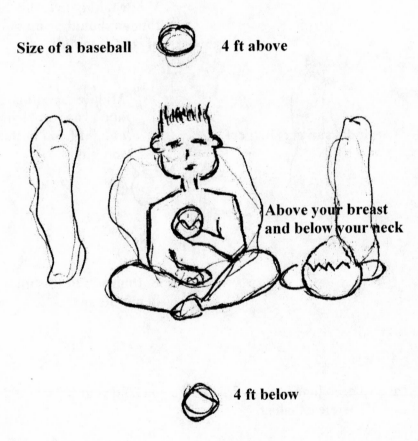

Size of a baseball   4 ft above

Above your breast
and below your neck

4 ft below

Visualize three suns.

Step 3

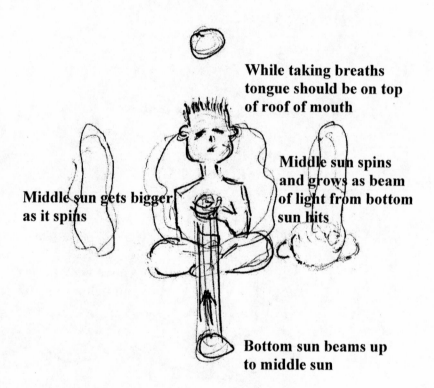

While taking breaths
tongue should be on top
of roof of mouth

Middle sun spins
and grows as beam
of light from bottom
sun hits

Middle sun gets bigger
as it spins

Bottom sun beams up
to middle sun

Take 10 deep/long breaths. Make sure you hold your breath for 2-3 seconds before exhaling.

Step 4

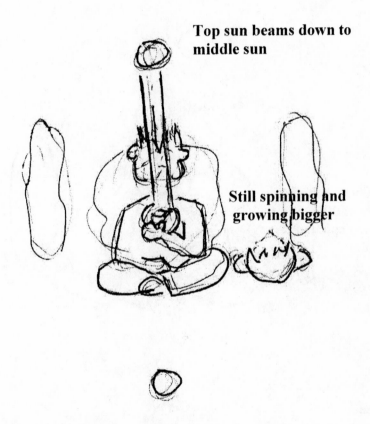

Top sun beams down to middle sun

Still spinning and growing bigger

Repeat step 1 and make sure the gates are still open. Take 10 deep/long breaths. Make sure you hold your breath for 2-3 seconds before exhaling.

Step 5

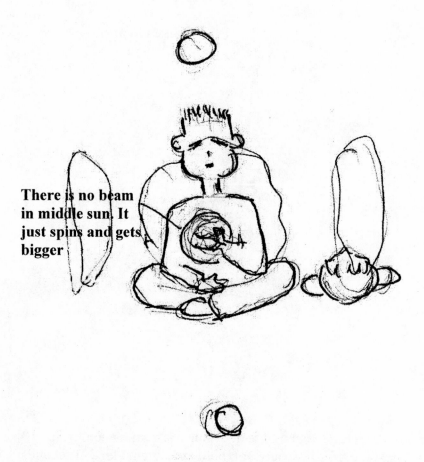

There is no beam
in middle sun. It
just spins and gets
bigger

Make sure the gates are still open. Take 10 deep/long breaths.
Make sure you hold your breath for 2-3 seconds before exhaling.

Step 6

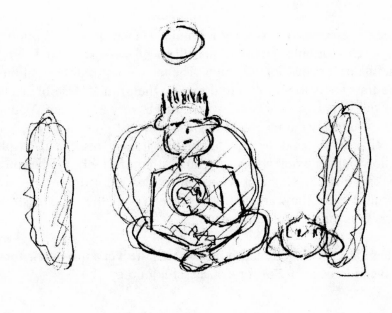

Cooling breaths start here. Make sure the gates are still open. Cool down by taking 50-60 regular breathing breaths. At this point the traveler should see the vortex or go through it.

* To wake the traveler up or bring him back tap his hands.

V. The Traveler

The traveler has a very easy job indeed. Their job is to simply get in a comfortable position and then place their hand on the facilitator's knew, leg, or thigh. The most comfortable position for the traveler is to simply lay down on the ground. Use blankets to lay on so that you are comfortable, this is very important. You may also use pillows under your ankles or to rest your arms on. When placing your hand on the facilitator, it may also help to place pillows under your arm so it can rest comfortably while you are making contact. Remember the whole idea is for the traveler to be comfortable. They are the VIP traveler and this is a first class ticket to spiritual enlightenment.

There are some do's and don'ts which are very important for the traveler to be aware of for a successful journey.

DO's

- DO close your eyes for lack of distraction (wearing a blindfold or placing something over the eyes can help)

- DO remove glasses (if you wear any)

- DO turn off your cell phone to minimize distraction

- DO remove all spare change, watches, belts, and anything metallic that may disturb the flow of energy

- DO relax as much as possible

- DO keep an open mind, and an open heart

- DO focus on love, and compassion

- DO trust yourself, the facilitator, and your guardians

- DO relax, and simply let it happen

This is pretty much it for the "DO's" section. Simply relax, and remove all items that could cause a possible distraction. Also, keep an open heart and mind, and feel love, compassion, and trust

DON'T

- DON'T eat at least 2 hours prior to traveling. Traveling on a full stomach can affect your concentration
- DON'T have any pre-conceived ideas or expectations
- DON'T bring any belief structures into your thought process. Beliefs cause expectations, and when they aren't met this causes doubt and disbelief.
- DON'T drink any alcohol, or take any drugs while traveling (you must be completely sober).

This pretty much covers all the basics that the traveler needs to know. Remember that you (as the traveler) are just an observer. Have courage, clarity, trust, love, and compassion during your travels. Always try to relax and just observe. Be 100 % honest about what you see, feel, hear, or experience. It may not make sense to you at the time but it will later down the road. Remember, you are accessing a level of existence you are not accustomed to.

You are only accustomed to this three-dimensional world which is governed by our five senses. Therefore until you become accustomed to Star Gate travel you can only interpret what you experience in your three-dimensional, five sense perspective. Again, be honest with yourself and with others about what you experience. This is a growing and learning process.

VI. The Observer Role

The observer role is a fairly simple one. They simply sit in the room and observe the facilitator and travelers. They are also there for the safety of both the facilitator and traveler(s). If for example, the facilitator is looking fatigued, or is slouching over, then the observer can come and gently straighten them out. If the facilitator looks like they are struggling to maintain, then observer can gently tap them out, and the facilitator can then awaken the traveler. Or if there are multiple facilitators who are facilitating 1 or more traveler(s) (which I will discuss later), then the observer can be the communicator between the facilitators. For example if one facilitator is done, he can signal to the observer who will gently tap out the other facilitator in order to end the session. So, basically, the Observer is there to simply observe and help where necessary. They should rarely touch the facilitators except for good cause, and should *never* touch the travelers. Touching the travelers can disturb their process of concentration, or it may pre-maturely bring them back from their travels.

Being an observer is also a great learning opportunity. You may sit in the room and observe the facilitators and study their various techniques. Each facilitator may have a different way of meditating and this is a great way to observe and learn. In addition, it is a wonderful opportunity to simply sit in the room and observe the energy. You can view the aura of the facilitators and travelers to gain an understanding of what exactly is occurring. The energy that fills the room can be very tangible and can be observed around the people and in the air. You may also sit and meditate, or just try to feel the energy that this active during a Star Gate session. Often times the room can heat up so much from all the energy that everyone begins to perspire.

So basically the observer does exactly that, which is to observe. At most they can assist with communication between multiple facilitators when ending a session, or, can assist a single facilitator if they begin to look fatigued. The role of the Observer is not necessary, but it can be a great assistance to the facilitator and travelers, and also a great learning opportunity for the observer themselves.

VII. The Re-Charging Method

The recharging method is used to give you energy prior to facilitation in case you need a boost. You can also use it after you're done facilitating if you feel drained or fatigued. In fact, you can use it any time you like. It is a good practice to recharge before and after any time you facilitate.

Preparation

1. Find a comfortable position to sit in. You may sit in a chair or on the ground kneeling, in a half lotus sitting position, or even laying down. The important thing is that you are comfortable, and try to keep your back straight.

2. Relax and close your eyes.

3. Now, visualize a sun, about the size of a basketball. Place this sun about 4-6 feet above you. Make sure you have a good idea of where the sun is and what it looks like. It can be any color or colors. Imagine it is radiating with light and energy.

4. Next, visualize another sun, again the size of a basketball. Place this sun 4-6 feet below you. Again, just be aware of where it is, and what color(s) you choose to make it. Imagine it is radiating with light and energy.

5. Now, visualize a 3rd sun. This sun is about the size of your fist and will be located in your higher chest area, between the 4th and 5th chakras. This area is often referred to as the soul seat. The color of this sun can also be any color(s).

6. Finally, visualize a 4th sun, right in the center of your brain where the hypothalamus gland is located. Make this one the size of your fist as well. (If you drew a line straight down from the top of your head, and a line straight back from your eyes, the intersect point is roughly where the hypothalamus gland is).

7. Touch your tongue to the roof of your mouth. This creates a circuit of energy and can help ground your energy during this exercise. It can be any part of your tongue making contact with any part of the roof of your mouth, as long as it is comfortable and not distracting.

*****

For the simplicity of explaining the following procedures, I will refer to each of the suns as follows:

1st Sun = Sun below you
2nd Sun = Soul Seat sun
3rd Sun = Hypothalamus gland
4th Sun = Sun Above you

*****

Lower Sun

8. Inhale slowly and deeply through your nose, and imagine that a beam of liquid light is beaming from the 1st sun (below you), straight into the 2nd sun

(soul seat). Imagine the 2nd sun rotating in the direction of your choice.

9. Hold your breath for 3-5 seconds and while you are holding your breath, imagine that the 2nd sun is collecting energy while continuing to rotate and radiate energy in all directions.

10. Now, bring both of your hands to the side of your head (do not touch your head) with the open palms facing towards your temples.

11. Exhale through your nose, and as you do imagine the liquid light energy pouring from the 2nd sun down your arms, out of your hands, and into the 3rd sun (hypothalamus). Imagine the 3rd sun rotating, collecting the energy, and radiating with light and energy.

12. You don't have to focus on, but, keep an awareness of the 3rd sun as you do your inhalations.

13. Do this 20 times

Higher Sun

14. Inhale through your nose, and imagine that a beam of liquid light is beaming down from the 4th sun (above you), straight into the 2nd sun (soul seat). Imagine the 2nd sun rotating in the direction of your choice.

15. Hold your breath for 3-5 seconds and while you are holding your breath, imagine that the 2nd sun (soul seat) is collecting energy while continuing to rotate and radiate energy in all directions.

16. Now, bring both of your hands to the side of your head (do not touch your head) with the open palms facing towards your head.

17. Exhale through your nose, and as you do imagine the liquid light energy pouring from the 2nd sun down your arms, out of your hands, and into the 3rd sun. Imagine the 3rd sun rotating, collecting the energy, and radiating with light and energy.

18. Again, always have an awareness of the 3rd sun, but focus on it during the exhalation.

19. Do this 20 times.

Final

The final part involves washing, cleansing, and re-charging your energy (aura) so that you are refreshed and re-vitalized.

20. Inhale, and imagine a beam of liquid energy from the 1st sun (lower sun) shooting straight up into your 3rd sun (hypothalamus).

21. Hold your breath for 3-5 seconds, and as you do imagine the 3rd sun gathering energy, rotating, and radiating both light and energy.

22. Exhale, and as you do imagine energy (any color) shooting out of the top of your head about 3-5 feet into the air, and then falling down all around you just like a water fountain. Imagine it cleansing your aura, your body, your organs, etc. Imagine yourself being immersed in this cleansing energy as it flows down over, around, and through you.

23. Do this 5-10 times. (The reason you do this not as many times, is that you do not want to become overcharged).

** Note that during this final cleansing method (the energy waterfall) you do not draw in energy from the sun above you, only from the sun below you.

Step 1

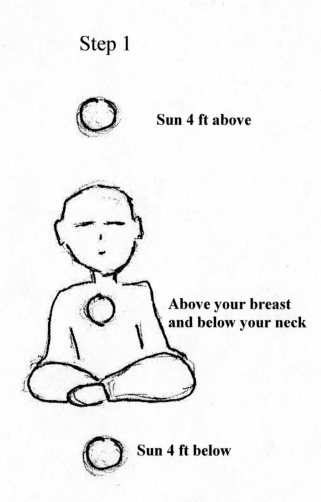

Sun 4 ft above

Above your breast
and below your neck

Sun 4 ft below

Visualize three suns about the size of a baseball.

Step 2

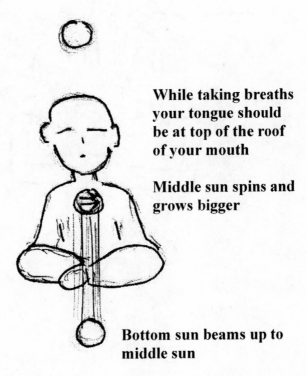

While taking breaths
your tongue should
be at top of the roof
of your mouth

Middle sun spins and
grows bigger

Bottom sun beams up to
middle sun

Take 10 deep/long breaths. Make sure you hold your breath 2-3
seconds before exhaling.

Step 3

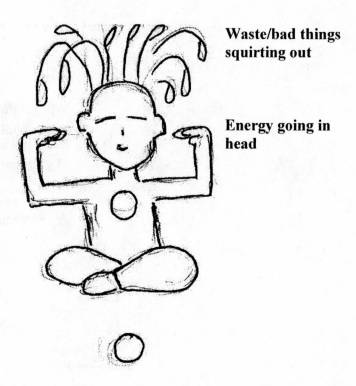

Waste/bad things squirting out

Energy going in head

When exhaling breath, direct hands toward head and imagine energy going through your head and all the waste/bad things squirting out of your head.

Step 4

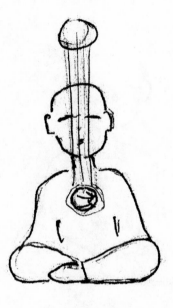

Top sun beams down to middle sun

Middle sun spins and grows bigger

Just like step 2, but the top sun beams down to the middle sun. Take 10 deep/long breaths. Make sure you hold your breath 2-3 seconds before exhaling. Then repeat step 3.

Step 5

This step requires the middle sun spinning and growing bigger while taking 10 deep/long breaths. Make sure you hold your breath 2-3 seconds before exhaling. Then repeat step 3.

VIII. Healing Method

The Star Gate method can also be used to conduct healing sessions. Sometimes a traveler will automatically experience healing energies while traveling. The mechanics, however, can be applied for direct and intentional healing. There are 2 very simple ways to do this. You may use this method to heal others, or to heal yourself.

1. Basic Meditation

The first way, is simply place your hands over or on the area you wish to heal. It doesn't matter if your hands are actually touching the body, but they can. Then, just do the mechanics for facilitating. Close your eyes, visualize the gates, ask your guardians for assistance, and then proceed with the mechanics of facilitating. After the cooling breaths are complete you can start again or simply end the session. The receiving person may or may not feel the energy transmitted depending on how sensitive they are to energies of a higher frequency. Most often there are sensations of heat, tingling, weightlessness, numbness, and/or pulses of energy moving through the body.

2. Recharging Method

The other way to conduct a healing session is to use the mechanics of recharging. Again, place your hands on or over the area you wish to heal and then go through the same methods as recharging. The only difference is that you're shooting the energy into the area you wish to heal (as opposed to into your hypothalamus gland). When you're done, still do the final step where you shoot the fountain of energy out the top of your head and cleanse both yourself and the person you're healing. The same sensations are felt using this method.

Both ways are fine to use, and neither one is wrong. You are simply using different techniques to channel the same healing energy. You don't need to imagine the area being healed or anything like that. Simply focus on the mechanics of transferring the energy, and it will automatically correct itself. Whatever is wrong will simply begin to correct itself, and if need be your guardians may assist you. The number of healing sessions depends on the injury or sickness you are trying to correct.

Remember that these are basic guidelines and you may learn and grow from them. Eventually you may find that you get better results with different techniques. You can even enhance the process, for example if you're a certified Reiki practitioner then use this method during your Reiki sessions. It is the exact same concept. The point is to use the basic methods given to you in this book, and as you learn and grow simply experiment with various techniques. This is just information, and like all information you should learn from it and then use what you learn to integrate with other information and concepts. Learning is a never ending process. The information in this book will help build a foundation for you to grow spiritually. Once that foundation is solid enough, you can start building upwards. There is no limit to how high you can build.

Step 1

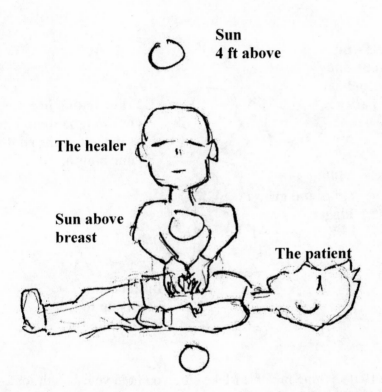

**Sun
4 ft above**

The healer

**Sun above
breast**

The patient

First off, place your hands where you feel the patient needs healing. Then imagine three Suns. One above your head, one above your breast and below your neck and one below you.

Step 2

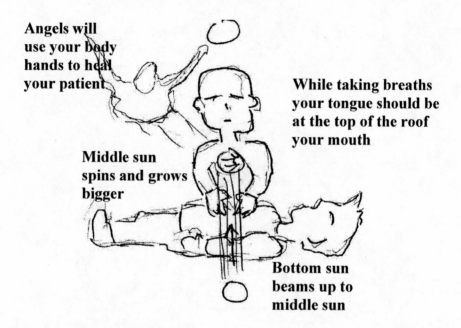

Angels will use your body hands to heal your patient

While taking breaths your tongue should be at the top of the roof your mouth

Middle sun spins and grows bigger

Bottom sun beams up to middle sun

Take 10 deep/long breaths. Make sure you hold your breath for 2-3 seconds before exhaling.

Step 3

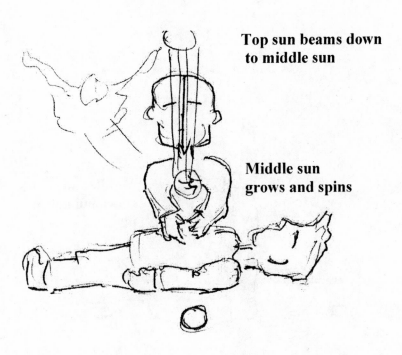

**Top sun beams down
to middle sun**

**Middle sun
grows and spins**

Just like step 2, but the top sun beams down to the middle sun.
Take 10 deep/long breaths. Make sure you hold your breath for 2-3
seconds before exhaling.

Step 4

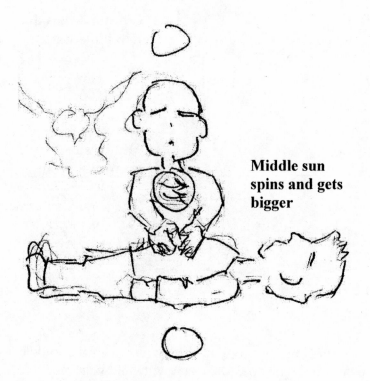

**Middle sun
spins and gets
bigger**

The middle sun spins and gets bigger as you take 10 deep/long breaths. Make sure you hold your breath for 2-3 seconds before exhaling. Patient should be healed or feeling better.

IX. Advanced Tips and Techniques

As you progress with your facilitating, traveling, and observing, you should make note of what works and what doesn't work. Learn from each other, use each other to brainstorm, learn, and grow together. So far, you have been given the mechanics of Star Gate travel. Now I will share with you various things that I have learned with one of my traveling teams. As you grow in number, you too will discover new ideas and techniques to experiment with.

The instructions you have been given this far are what you need to get going. Practice them with consistency and perseverance. Once you get a feel for the entire process, you may experiment with what works best for you. For example, maybe you find it easier to visualize a cube, or swirling vortex, instead of a sun. Also, perhaps you find that you travel better under certain conditions (in the morning, after meditation, while incense is burning, etc.). Find what works best for you, but do not stray from the basic mechanics, and as always use common sense and have an awareness of safety.

This being said, here are some advanced tips and techniques that one of my traveling teams and I have discovered.

Variations in posture/positioning

Some facilitators find it easiest to simply sit in a half lotus position on the ground, with hands on their knees, palms up, with the tips of the thumb and forefinger touching. This is the traditional posture for meditation. Other facilitators find it more effective to sit cross legged. Others use hand motions to draw energy from the lower sun up into their soul seat, and down from the higher sun into their soul seat. There is no right or wrong way, just as long as you discover what works best for you. Remember, no matter what facilitation techniques you try, always keep your tongue touching the roof of your mouth for maximum effect.

Multiple facilitators and travelers

Once you have tried facilitating 1-2 people, you may increase the experience however you wish. For example, try having 2 facilitators, with just one traveler. This will help enhance the experience from some travelers. Also, you may create a link of several facilitators and travelers. This allows for more people to experience Star Gate travel at the same time. It also acts as a great way for the energy to be dispersed between the facilitators so one person does not get as fatigued. You may use as many people as you wish, just remember there must be an unbroken chain of direct contact.

Variation in traveling conditions

Some travelers, we found, tend to travel better in complete silence. If you find this is the case, try experimenting with ear plugs. Also, we found that some people tend to relax better, and travel better in complete darkness. Try traveling through the Star Gate at night, or, in a dark room. You can even go a step further and use blindfolds. Whatever works best for the traveler, remember, they are the VIP on these journeys. Make them as comfortable and relaxed as possible.

Mantras

Use a mantra or chant when you're the traveler in order to help quiet your mind and increase your meditative state. One very well known mantra is "Aum" (pronounced Oh-M). You can simply chant this by itself. You may get different results if you elongate the "oh" or the "m" sound. You can also add the word to anything you like, for example Aum + peace, and chant that. Adding the word Aum to your mantra will help enhance it.

Your soul mantra is the sound vibration that was used to breathe you into existence. It is the sound that your aura makes as it vibrates, and is your unique signature upon all levels of existence. Your soul mantra is to you, as your fingerprints are to your body. They are your unique signature. All soul mantras begin with the commonly known mantra "Aum". Use your Soul Mantra while you facilitate or as you travel. It will increase the intensity of your experience.

If you do not know your Soul Mantra, then use any simple mantra of your choosing. But, always begin with "Aum". So for example, your mantra can be "Aum Kosol" (your first name). Or, it can be "Aum Love Courage". It can even be something as random as "Aum Rock Smelly Cat". Whatever you choose, just remember that it begins with "Aum", and your intent is to grow, learn, and share your experiences with an open heart and mind. You can ask your guardians what your soul mantra is while your traveling, the answer will come to you.

It is a good idea to do any chanting in your head so it is not distracting. But, if you find that it helps you and/or your particular group then by all means chant out loud.

Cooling Breaths

The cooling breath portion of facilitation is the most intense part of the energy transfer process. For some reason, within my experience, the cooling breath always yields the most intense and vivid experiences for the traveler(s). We experimented by increasing the number of cooling breaths. For example, instead of 20 breaths from below, 20 from above, 20 holding, and 20 cooling breaths, we changed the amount. We tried 7 breaths from below, 7 from above, 7 holding breaths, and 50 cooling breaths. The results were phenomenal, and people experienced much more intense travel. Some who have never traveled until that point were instantly sent through the Star Gate, experiencing vivid visions and sensations. This can be an intense technique, so use it only after you have practiced the basic methods.

Spiritual Guidance

Never lose sight of the fact that your guardians are always present. Do not hesitate to ask for help when facilitating or traveling. Sometimes if someone is having trouble traveling, it is as simple as asking your guardians for guidance, protection, and assisted travel. When facilitating, your guardians can always be called upon for support and assistance as well. Be receptive to the roles they play, and ask for whatever is needed to ensure a safe and successful journey. Never forget to thank them, and have trust in the help they will provide you.

Breath Retention

Breath retention is an important part of the basic mechanics, and we have found that the longer you hold your breath (comfortably), the more energy you can gather. Starting out at a comfortable pace is what's important, and as you become skilled in the meditative methods you'll simply be able to hold your breath longer and longer.

No Touch Facilitation

After a facilitator has enough experience facilitating, they will become a powerful conductor of energy. Some individuals can facilitate travel without direct contact. This is accomplished because the facilitator's aura will act as the conductor, which in turn transfers the energy to the traveler via their aura. This is a great way for one facilitator to facilitate multiple people. This can even be used over long distances, all the facilitator needs to do is set a time with the traveler and then visualize the traveler. You can visualize them in detail, or, simply as an energy body. It is important to symbolize their uniqueness to create contact, so one easy way is just to imagine they have a name tag with their name on it. As long as there is an agreement between facilitator and traveler, and the facilitator imagines the traveler (in whichever way works), then long distance facilitation can be initiated. Again, this is due to the nature of existence and the fact that everything is made of energy. You're simply opening up a pathway between your two energies.

Opening eyes while traveling

Opening your eyes while traveling allows you to see the energy in action. The room or area becomes so charged that the energy can actually be seen. Some people will notice waves of energy coming off the facilitator, the various layers of the aura, or even the presence of their guardians. The more you travel, the more sensitive you become to higher frequencies of energy. As this becomes apparent, traveling with your eyes open is a great way to witness what is happening. It is a great reminder that Star Gate traveling is just a way to experience multidimensional existence and this can be done at any point during your waking or sleeping state. It's a great way for people to validate what they are experiencing, and bring their awareness of existence to the next level.

Self Facilitation

If you wish to travel, and have no one to facilitate you, then facilitate yourself! Just go through the basic mechanics of facilitation, and that's it. The energy may not be as intense compared to normal travel, because during normal travel you're just relaxing with your eyes closed rather than focusing on the mechanics. But, depending on the person it could be even better than normal travel. Remember, it just depends. Everyone is unique, so try everything and see what works best for you.

Pyramids

The Star Gate method was designed for optimum effect in conjunction with a pyramid structure. The pyramid serves as an amplifier of energy and a means to intensify the Star Gate method. Engaging in Star Gate travel or healing while inside a pyramid structure will contain, channel, and intensify the experience. We are currently creating a non-profit organization where we intend to build a Star Gate center that contains a pyramid. Here, people will be able to come and Star Gate, meet, learn, and grow.

(See the "Pyramid Building" section on my website for more information about pyramid structures) The website address is:

http://www.homestead.com/_allaboutlife

Psychic Pulse/Energy Harnessing

Finally, you can use these techniques to harness energy for whatever purpose you wish. Use the recharging method, and then cup your hands and shoot the energy into your hands. Do this several times until you feel a numbness or pressure building, and then form it into a ball. You can project this energy across the room for example, and with enough practice you can make things move. It takes practice, concentration, and creative visualization. Play around with the energy around you, and see what you can make it do. This is the next step to harnessing the Star Gate knowledge, but that is for another book…..

X. Safety

Safety and common sense is always important no matter what you do, and this is no exception. I've already mentioned some of the basic rules such as not to suddenly awaken a traveler during their travel, and not to touch their head. Also, this may seem obvious, but never get up and leave while you are facilitating. The traveler needs guidance through the entire process. This has happened before, and luckily the traveler was able to awaken by themselves with some help from their guardians. Again, just follow the guidelines in this book and use common sense.

Another thing worth mentioning is to sustain your own health and environment. The more you travel, the more you will begin to ascend spiritually. If you don't maintain your health then you won't advance as fast spiritually. Your body is a vehicle for the experience and the vehicle only runs as good as you care for it.

It is also a good idea to practice Star Gating in the same area or room, and to keep this area clean. Keep the area uncluttered and clean in order to sustain a healthy environment which is conducive to travel. Other ways to keep the energy in a room clean and clean is to keep plants, water, burn incense, etc. Feng Shui is the practical application of this concept. Try researching it in your spare time, it is a great way to supplement the Star Gate meditation.

One final note is to re-iterate the importance of being consistent. In other words, once you practice this method, continue to do so on a consistent basis. When you access other realms of existence, you are opening an energetic pathway back to yourself. It is just like driving down a road you've never traveled. While traveling you are always in the protection of your guardians, and the meditative methods are naturally attuned to higher, healing, positive vibrations. So, if you go down a new road you are subject to come in contact with whatever is on that road be it good or bad. If you choose to stop Star Gating, these roads are still open. Therefore, if you then begin to participate in activities that lower you own energy vibration (smoking, drinking, drugs, lack of exercise, stress, negative thoughts, negative emotional reactions, etc.) and do not balance it out, you will be subject to contact with entities that exist on lower vibrations. This could vary from energetic parasites, to various forms of possession. This is a worst case scenario, possession that is, and is not meant to scare you away from practice. Just remember that you are simply experiencing life with a greater awareness, and just like in three dimensional awareness you must stay healthy or suffer the consequences. This is very important to keep in mind.

XI. Traveler's Experiences

Some of the members from one of my traveling teams have shared their experiences in a forum online. I wanted to share some of their experiences and they have agreed to allow them to be shared. Names will be left out, however, these are direct clippings from posts made by people I have facilitated, have self facilitated themselves, or were facilitated by someone else (other than me). These examples are just a very small sampling of the various experiences that people have had. These experiences are very basic and introductory in nature and will help give you an idea of what other people experience and how they interpret it. Don't limit your expectations based on these experiences. Some people have been able to speak with their guardians consistently, others have experienced intense physical sensations and healings, others have been able to speak to relatives that have passed on, and some can even travel to various places at will. Remember, the possibilities are endless and these are just to get your started. The following are excerpts from various postings and they can be viewed in full online in the Star Gate forum (mentioned in the "Networking" chapter). The grammar has not been edited so that each experience is communicated in its original form.

Experiences

"i traveled for an hour this evening. i made it through 3 breaths when i started to see and feel some white rings pulsing towards my face. i continued breathing normally after that and i could feel my mind slipping deeper and deeper.. i eventually felt this heavy energy coming out of me. very strange feeling heavy energy. usually the energy i feel is very lite and i feel like i'm floating.. this kind of energy was grounding and i could feel it floating around my head... i ended up looking into the darkness and seeing a bunch of buildings in a village and what looked like a castle.. i set my cell phone alarm and it rang at that point.. i did some recharging before and after.."

"Well, I self star gated last night. I've actually been trying self star gating for awhile, before Kosol brought it up. Each time, I've had the same sensations I've had while Star Gate traveling. That is, I always feel charged & energized, like my body feels lighter & more ... well, it's hard to describe. Like at times I can actually feel myself vibrating, as a whole, but down to the smallest particle. I've also had sensations where I feel like I'm floating in complete nothingness, I lose awareness of physical sensation, but retain awareness of consciousness. Last night, when I was doing the 10, 10, 10 cycle, I saw stars everywhere, just like I was looking up in the sky (my eyes were closed). I was moving my head to scan the sky, and there some of the stars were flashing different colors & then would move & form patterns. I have no idea what it meant, but it was pretty vivid. After that, I just kind of fell asleep during the cooling breaths."

"well, i self stargated to day after my 3o minute of recharging , then i did 40 minute of stargate, i feel floating and saw lots of multi-color light , and i was moving or having the sensation of moving faster and faster.the multi color light got brighter and brighter. i feel floating lighter and lighter , it is fun then i saw the gate itself it look like multi ring with in a ring it was huge. and was gold , green and blue, purple , and reds. it was awsome then the guarding come into my experience they look like light as they are. and saw [said] , having fun yet? i couldn't helped but to laught and lost my concentration and returned back to my normal auric sight. and still laughting . that was my experience , so i thank the guardians for thier sense of humor."

"It looked like I was starring into the sky. I tried to stay focused on one point and hold it. When I was finally focused, I saw many shadows surrounding me. One moved closer than the rest. It was right next to me. I got a chill, but wasn't scared. I was excited! Looks like I'm moving forward!"

"I felt like I was there in the room the whole time, but Kosol said I was out like a light. Snoring like a mother. I felt like my breaths were calm and quite., but they weren't. I felt alot of energy at my hands, and a floating sensation. I couldn't fell Kosol's leg. He said there was alot of activity with the hand on his knee. I had a single visual which was the face of a baby. It was clear and I saw it before. There was tapping on my hand which I noticed right before I was tapped out"

"I self facilitated after getting home from work, for about 1 hour. After I started the upper sun cycle (I was doing 15,15,15, 100), I just lost concsiousness.... it always seems to happen during the upper sun cycle. All I remember after that, was a feeling like I'm falling, and I woke up. My hand hit my chest (i was lying down with my arms at my side) so I either twitched, or, my hand somehow got above my chest and just fell when I woke up. This happened 3 times... the sensation of fallin, and my hand(s) hitting my chest. Each time I was jarred awake... and each time, my energy stabilized like i was grounding again after I woke up. After I woke up each time, my whole body felt a tingling sensation, and for some reason a lot of energy came into my mouth & especially in my tongue, it felt numb. I noticed when I released my tongue from the roof of my mouth the feeling would go away, but when I touched it again the feeling re-charged. No visuals or audio, but, definitely physical sensations."

"i remember feeling energy all over and seeing pulses of energy. after that I recharged and self facilitated. into drawing energy from my upper sun i thought i saw my guardians and then on my cooling breath's felt the feeling of being pulled forward, almost like i wanted to slump over or fall over and i got this visual of almost like traveling warp speed on Star Trek. i saw what i thought was stars or little different colored light traveling past me at a very high rate of speed, almost to as if i was traveling through a vortex or worm hole. after that it started to rain really loud and i lost my focus.."

XII. Conclusion

The Star Gate method is the short path to spiritual awakening. It is intended to speed up the evolution of the planet and allow for a direct experience so people can have the proof they need to begin or continue their spiritual re-discovery. It can be used for healing, exploration, personal growth, relaxation, and learning. Remember the ultimate intent, however, which is to allow anyone and everyone to experience firsthand the things that ascended masters have been attempting to communicate since the dawn of time. That is, the nature of existence and our nature as spiritual beings. The time for communication has been replaced by the need for experience.

As you try the techniques and being your travels, please share your experiences in the Star Gate forum, and on the traveler's forum. That information is in the "Networking" chapter. Also, feel free to share any new techniques or discoveries. The purpose is to share this knowledge to keep the project growing so more and more people can reap the benefits from these techniques.

This is the end of the Star Gate methods and mechanics, and contains everything you need to get started. This conclusion marks a beginning. A new beginning of spiritual enlightenment that has already begun on the planet. Keep an open heart, open mind, and share this information with everyone you know. Information is meant to be shared so we as a species can grow and learn together. The more we share, the more dynamic our growth and learning will be. I wish you happy and safe travels, and nothing but the best in all you do and become.

XIII. Networking

As you form groups or have individual experiences, feel free to network with other people that use these techniques. In fact, network with people that don't use these techniques and share them wherever you go.

There are a couple places I would like to invite you to visit. One is my website which has been up for several years. The address is:

http://www.homestead.com/_allaboutlife

I invite everyone to check out all the information on this site. This is where you can find information on the pyramid structures mentioned in chapter 9. Also, there is a link on the main page called "Stargate Ascension Project". Click on that and browse the material in that section. There is a section with illustrations of the meditation techniques.

There is also a forum that we actively discuss this information in which is called "Stargateascension – Stargate Ascension Project". You can view the messages by going to my website, clicking on the "Stargate Ascension Project" link from the main page, and then clicking on "IX. Traveler's Logbook Forum". This will bring you to the message threads.

Feel free to subscribe to this discussion form, to share your experiences and interact with other people practicing these techniques. To subscribe simply send an email to the following address and request to join the forum:

Stargateascension-subscribe@yahoogroups.com

You will receive an email when your subscription is confirmed. There is no cost, this is completely free. I hope to see you on there.

XIV. Travel Journal

As you begin your travels and experiences it is a good idea to keep a journal. This way you have a documented reference which is a great way to observe your own progress, recall past experiences, and share your information with others. Be as accurate as possible with your entries, and pay attention to all the smallest details. This way you can identify various ways to experiment and try new things.

Here is a suggested format for your journal entries, but of course you can use whatever works best for you.

Date:
Time:
Location:
Conditions:
Facilitator(s):
Traveler(s):

Experience:

Notes:

XV. Author's Note

This book in its entirety was written by Gerald (Jerry) Evans II. The information is intended to be provided from the perspective and intents of Kosol Ouch. Jerry Evans wrote the book in order to maximize the quality of the information since English is not Kosol Ouch's native language.

The techniques and methods are originally the property of Kosol Ouch. There was relevant material that was added by Jerry throughout the creation of this book, as both Jerry and Kosol continuously added to the information based on their experiences and insights. All material was reviewed and approved by Kosol Ouch prior to publication. This book is a result of their collaborative efforts in presenting the desired information in the desired context.

Printed in the United States
50052LVS00005B/67-72